**Calling Myself
On The Phone**

Previous publications
Riding Shotgun (Smith/Doorstop Books 1987)
What The Snow Believes (Scratch 1992)
Invisible Mending (Ure Group Press 1994)
Mee-Mawing (Tarantula 1996)

No Man's Land (with Jean Sprackland, photos by Dave Walker, Cheetah Books 2002). Exhibited at the Lowry Centre, Salford, January–April 2002.
Desire Paths (Fuggygug Films, directed by Sarah Jane Eyre)

Acknowledgements
Thanks are due to the editors of the following publications in which some of these poems have appeared: *Fire, Dreamcatcher, The Language of Conversation* (Routledge), *The New Writer, The North, Other Poetry, Passing Clouds, Pennine Platform, Prop, Rain Dog, The Rialto, Rustic Rub, Seam, Stand, Staple, Verse, www.slope.org.*

Calling Myself On The Phone

Steven Waling

Smith/Doorstop Books

Published 2003 by
Smith/Doorstop Books
The Poetry Business
The Studio
Byram Arcade
Westgate
Huddersfield HD1 1ND

Copyright © Steven Waling 2003
All Rights Reserved

ISBN 1-902382-48-X

Steven Waling hereby asserts his moral right to be identified as the author of this book.

British Library Cataloguing-in-Publication Data. A catalogue record for this book is available from the British Library.

Typeset at The Poetry Business
Printed by Peepal Tree, Leeds

Cover photo © Dave Walker, entitled 'Feature Window' from his sequence 'Birds Don't Sing in the Dark'

Distributed by Central Books Ltd, 99 Wallis Road, London E9 5LN

The Poetry Business gratefully acknowledges the help of Kirklees Metropolitan Council and Yorkshire Arts.

CONTENTS

9	Early Rock & Roll
10	To Convulsions
11	Power Cuts
12	'My Hen Had A Haddock'
13	What I Did On My Holidays
14	Pink Flesh
15	For John Peel
16	Kind of Blue
18	What She Said
19	Recessive
20	North
21	Searching For Edwin
22	Sharpie's Boot
23	Winter Sales
24	Ferris: From The Top:
25	The Great Wall of Todmorden
26	Why The Sea
27	Missed The Bus
28	Getting Home Before You Left
29	National Express
30	The Trouble With Being A Dog
31	After Wordsworth
32	New York, Paris
33	Lunch Poem
34	Starting With A Line By Declan MacManus
35	Mobile
36	Night Before

37	The Cloud People
38	Figures
39	Accosted By Angels
40	You Hated The Film
41	Tired
43	Shifting Furniture
44	Simple
45	Like The First Morning
46	Ironing Your Top
47	Every Day Is Like Sunday
48	Letters To The Editor

Patiently Waiting	48
La Vache Enragé	49
Grateful Citizen	50
Ornithologist	51
Blue Forever	52

54	Make-Over
55	The Suitcase
56	Lost
57	Grey
58	A Sea Change
59	Early Communion
60	Godtalk
61	Seen The Light
62	Room With A View
63	Desire Paths
64	On Light:

'Sometimes I'd like to call myself on the phone and tell myself to shut up' – Miles Davies

'Anecdote, anecdote. And is every anecdote a meeting ground for strangers?' – Nicholas Moore

Early Rock & Roll
1958

Because at the moment of birth
my synapses buzzed
at the frequency of long-since erased
stations in Memphis or Duluth

I jitterbugged
straight out of the womb
to some glass confinement of tubes
and wires. My limbs cut a rug

to the hand-jive, my body
shook, rattled, rolled;

and with one of those odd
twists of fate I'm told
happens in these cases, my first
LP was Bill Haley's.

To Convulsions

What knocked me off that wall,
Superman with a duffel coat for a cape?
One minute running out of the bogs,
the next on a table with faces
I dreamed were devils, more
scared of me than I was of them.
What electric surges blew my fuse
on the lawn when I was three?

Only you, making me jumpy and odd,
putting drawing pins on my chair.
The reason I've never learnt to swim,
you could tap me on the shoulders
any time you liked, and I just
learned how to fall, not knowing if
I spasmed, shook, or turned blue:

there's still small gaps in my head
from those visits you paid at night.
Though you came so seldom I almost
forgot my little white pills, you could
still send monsters to my daydreams
when I'd wake woozy, bruised as a drunk
with the rest of the day off school.

Power Cuts

Dads have their own armchairs
even dogs won't sit in. Evenings
are smoking, reading aloud
from the paper in a voice

like a tape running slow. The clock,
plugged to the wall, doesn't tick
and air tastes of tobacco inside
and out. Someone hands out candles

for later as TV brings news from
the Street. Soft lad from school
goes upstairs, changes out of uniform,
as Dad's little factory rolls out fags.

Today's tea is nostalgia, with chips,
tomorrow's the same with mash.
Mum and the dog asleep. Soft lad's
in his bedroom reading all night

what fresh air will taste of someday.

'My Hen Had A Haddock'

Write down tonight's homework then it's RE.
We reach the miracle of the coin in the fish's mouth
before it's English: Henry IV Pt One,
Mrs Wallwork slopes down to cottage and pension,
believes in nothing much. Everything important

lasts for an hour then History. Did Grandad
teach Christ that trick with coins? A bird flies in
through the window and out, takes my life
and the essays not handed in, or done, along with it.
I don't learn much just get up in darkness,

trudge through snow to sing 'Men of Harlech'
as the head drones through the *Imitation of Christ*.
Someone drawing-pins my chair as I ponder
the nature of things in Latin, vocab
at the back of the book. Falstaff scoffs capon

in the hall that smells of old polish and pumps.
God's a cashmere sweater round the lovely
shoulders of Miss Green; then Games:
I forgot my kit, again, deliberate they say,
drag me fully clothed to the showers; or Panhead,

Double Maths, measures my hair, says 'Get it cut!'
at the end of the corridor where someone's
always waiting for the strap. Behind the gym
High School girls teach Physics to Grammar boys.
I have it bad or good but won't be invited.

Then home at half three to a future that is always
exams, facts off the board: like Bismarck
and the Entente Cordiale: amo, amas. That
trick coin: five years then out through the gates
where no-one remembers: table, O table.

What I Did On My Holidays

There was a horse in it. Sheep
penned in by a high iron fence
and a locked refinery gate. Clouds,
where the sky hung its lip at me,
hands in my pockets and peevish
on a headland of great escapes
and winds overacting on the cliffs.

I was in the wrong skin, under canvas
on a wet Bank Holiday, so I trailed
behind the family as we walked
to Heysham and back. The part
of my brain with a horse in it
galloped West over Morecambe Bay
like the Lone Ranger, dodging the
quicksands and arguments as I rode
my own shadow over the cliffs.

Pink Flesh

Scrubbed, clean, just out of the bath:
like she's sleeping on a bed of silk.

Two years on, almost to the week,
his hands crossed in front like your father
giving his daughter away:
trying to remember his lines;
the pair of them dressed to the nines
like in life they never were.

Him in shirtsleeves watching the wrestling,
her baking rock cakes in the back
is how I'd choose to remember
if it weren't for the sight of pink flesh
in uncomfortable cloth, both of them together
absconded from their own funerals.

For John Peel

He's stuck with revision and the radio
as an ambulance delivers its parcel
past his window. Up seventeen floors
he could fly back home
if he wanted. You're the only one visits

this time of night. He tries to pray
to a blank wall, then coffee. New Order,
the Fall: he tapes your songs. Surgeons
unwrap the occupants of trolleys
down the road in the hospital

as he attempts half-arsed half-hearted
to join some club the human race
joined yesterday. The festive 50:
everyone else designs chemical plants
till two in the morning, writes up

notes on anatomy, and our hero
writes ambulance verse, can't hear
the knock on the door. Two miles away
someone's sorted between white sheets
as your voice miscues an EP.

Kind of Blue
for Elizabeth

The sky at this hour of the day –
blue of old jeans fades to grey
over the Central Library. An office
from the sixties: white. Time shapeless,

warm as alphabet soup. I drink
cappuccino in the Gallery Cafe
as an old man at the counter takes
a blue Queen's head from his wallet,

and read how this city's a circuit
diagram of streets superimposed over
vascular systems of blue veins
remembered only on old maps.

Take, for instance, the hollow culvert of
Tib Street, no longer flowing. Thoughts
are riverine, pleased with themselves
but blue, damp as old warehouses full

of cotton goods. If I were to walk
to the Cathedral, the ghost of the Dene
might haunts its way under Hanging Ditch
a shadow of its blue self. Or I could

trace the route of some old watercourse
back to its source in the marshes
tramped through by invading Romans
blue with cold and ague. But today

walks to the gallery to stare at
canvases exploding like fireworks

of a Festival to the God of Lights.
This year has made me kind of blue

but the rain threatening overhead
negotiates for blue sky and sun
from the Indian summer blazing off
municipal walls. It seems for months

I've been walking in a field
of deep grace, searching for colour:
here it is, green blue yellow red
lifting me briefly to speechlessness.

What She Said

Didn't have any pain. More an ache
across my shoulders, down my left arm.
Dad wanted me so I joined the Rechabites.
Mind, I didn't fancy life without a drink.

Knew what it was. I'd read all about it,
and seen it. *True posterior infarct*, that's
what they wrote. I met Eunice through
them: we used to swap each other's clothes.

You could have wrung me out like a dishcloth.
Never knew I'd so much sweat. Anyway, it
weren't as if I ever drank much. Still, I once
won a poetry book, the sort I like that rhymed.

I always have to be different. Your dad
was in agony, not me: nothing. Well anyway,
now Eunice walks sideways down stairs, fat,
can hardly get out the door. I don't like salad,

and she does. I've got bruises all up my legs,
one right up here. Don't know what from.
Did I tell you I fainted on the coach
from Blackpool? They said I couldn't even

have a medicinal rum. One of those things.
It's not as if I ever ate. I mean, you're
just going along and … not even a nip.
So anyway, I decided to leave the Rechabites.

Recessive

It's when someone you ought to know
talks about an uncle, no more than a whippet,
who stopped with a hand to the throat
his father from beating his mother.

Or it's that cousin of your mother's
unmentioned till, visiting your dad
at the cemetery, she happens on his grave
(who killed himself before you were born).

Or those three cousins who don't exist
till one has the snip, and appears in the paper
as one of the Port Stanley heroes:

it's the silence, gaps in narrative,
this history of not looking back
she's kept at the back of a drawer.

And she's at it again Sunday lunch:
how afterwards, he never touched her
but always wanted things his way

till the business collapsed
and everyone left him alone.

North

It's where I live. Searchlighting
streets, the night owl
meets the hawk taking over
in the trees across the way.

Round here the landscape's
moon. I need some sun. I live above
a café by the coach stop. Each morning
I need your dawn in my face.

Drivers in from trawling the towns
patted my head, knocked me sideways
on that spot by the side of the road,
signed my leg in its plaster.

A dent in my knee the shape
of a car-park. Life shone
a torch in my eyes: born there
but long since moved away.

Searching For Edwin

> *'Wi mi' yed i' my hat, an' mi feet i' my shoes
> I'm fain to be toddlin' whoam.'* – Edwin Waugh

Where my head hares off to when the hound's
at my heels: under cover of cloudscape
I walk to F'ow Edge Farm, where a curlew
calls for company or to be left alone
and sheep chew edges off the moor.

I'm searching the paths our Edwin trod:
caught in the cleft of an unexpected fork;
this way ruins, that the reservoir and well
bubbling like an argument from stone,
I go the wrong then the right way, end up
losing him on paths that lead nowhere.

Sunspots, global warming or a simple
downturn in weather brings the hail
to freeze my face in April; I turn into it,
hear the Dene Layrocks whistling psalms:
How can we sing the Lord's song
on a corner where nobody listens.
They march down famine paths out of view

so I follow Edwin's feet to Waterfoot:
den, lair, bolthole from debtors; his slice
of Chorley cake all currents and pastry.
Where the Irwell careens past disassembled
mills: girders and walls broke, floorless,
I realise I won't be back for the encore
of chimney stacks and looms that once
beat out an almost remembered hymn.

Sharpie's Boot

Sir Francis Sharp Powell, Baronet, MP, green as lawns,
as the leaves of Mesnes Park sycamores,
or the scum on the duck pond: whoever sat him here
in the open has made him look all queasy.

Erected by public subscription, he stares over our heads,
seems always about to speak to pigeons and flower beds
on the evils of drink, the health of the miners,
or the message from the pulpit of the church

seen from Rivington Pike. Unseen brass bands
play 'God Save The Queen' as we rub his boot,
run round three times for luck.
He evades the questions with silence. No one

gets statues for nothing. Even the yeomanry, forgotten
in a corner of the park, got theirs for the Boer War.
They'll steal anything these days, and now it's just a space,
like the holes where mines once were. A useless wheel

stands outside the college down the road.
Dreams sink and still they polish his boots
as if he'll rise, walk into town and make
the speech that makes us young again.

Winter Sales

I buy a pair of pants, three quid off.
They're none too tight, I'll need a belt.
Blank with turnups. Start again.

I buy a pait of keks. That's better.
Locally-coloured chinos with a belt.
Won't anyone sleep with me? Aren't they

tight enough? I might grow into them
if I was ten going on eleven. I'm not,
I'm thirty six. Same age as my belt size.

These are 38's. I'm not growing younger.
I'm reading magazines that take poetry
seriously. All the books I've spent my life

not reading: Huysman's *A Rebours*, Proust,
The Collected Works of Robert Southey.
I also missed *Henry: Portrait of*

a Serial Killer: wanting to take an axe
to English Lit will only get blood
on my new pants. In a parallel universe,

I get to finish *The Faerie Queene*.
But that way lie pants that fit, a job
firing *The Western Canon* at college kids

and madness. In this world, I wear a belt,
a good strip of leather round the waist.
You get one life. Buy your trousers tight.

Ferris: From The Top:

dark roofs, arcades, something hazy at the edge
of the picture: down to tiles, numbered like the hairs
on your head. This is the plan that is no plan, surrounded
by ring roads, circular as a spinning wheel

that touches earth then climbs through a day when wind
spins you round the stones of a gallery, over the dome
of the Corn Exchange, past bijou shops, restaurants.
There's grass on ledges, pigeons roosting on eaves

unseen by punters in the fair. Dazzled by the glare off
glass facades, what strikes you is the breadth of it stretched
into greys, reds, where a strip of blue denotes canal; no green
but the cloud's low. Besides, you're not up long enough

before descending to duff German pop, then back into space
and the catch of your breath for the last revolution.
Now it's just you and the wind, Leeds nowhere,
but coming up as the wheel slows down, the ride ends

and you step onto a shaking world, its solid geometry
of street names pinned to the walls as you pass.

The Great Wall of Todmorden

Overrun Saturdays by barbarous hordes
up from Manchester to the third round
cup tie at Leeds but they don't even stop
just run through on the train. We live
with mystery but don't like the feeling.
It endures: a pair of Levi's just holding
together. At lock gates, obsessive-compulsive
water falls in strands or ropes into the dark
twist of canal, refreshing itself slowly – almost,
sometimes, poisonously – into the mind.

An abstract sculpture (title: Bridge)
badly widened feels the proximity
of the unknown. First the road came,
then canal, and no one gives anything
away. Things unfold with a rapidity
that's thrilling: water's polished shield
is copper not brass, of which not much
– the great unknowable walls knocked down,
rebuilt, patched, falling again and failing
better like Beckett in his trench coat.

Why The Sea

would recall Michelangelo
is anyone's guess but the way
it chips, bites, clawhammers
cliffs in a doomed attempt
at definition's a striking
reminder of those carved slaves'
aborted escape from white
Cararra chains. Never done
with its continuous gnawing
at chalk, the rain sends the hotel
we stayed in for the Storm Drain
Manufacturers' Conference
teetering over the edge for
non-payment of rent. Look,
I've spotted the headboard that
witnessed our first tossing
and turning nights away from
respective husbands and wives:
we watched it dredged into drift-
wood washed like us onto shores
of some notional coast where
every beach is thick with flotsam
and jetsam, stuff thrown over
when the sea muscled in on us
like a landlord reviewing
his crumbling seaside properties.

Missed The Bus

Bones cold as twigs. Dark: someone
has missed the last bus, still two miles
to go. Is this your life, in the file marked
'Awaiting Reference', stacked in a room

in the basement with the rest of your stuff?
Each step returns you to the central heating
and catfood smells. Bored windows blink
their curtains; nothing fazes this time of night:

not the bluebottle taxis, nor clouds coming
to greet them with a wet kiss on the lips.
Hello, dark night of the soul and a bird
seeking its way out of your head.

Hello to the drizzle. What shall it do,
this gift you can't give back? Desperate,
a dog wrapped in the parcel of himself,
you reach home soaked, key in door,

find sleep sitting up, waiting for you.

Getting Home Before You Left

The night's as old as who it feels. You feel
ancient as your car trawls the outskirts,
factories, retail parks. In the driver's seat
you have my sympathy with those CD's:
Pavarotti, Dire Straits, *Cats*. Society won't
make an emergency stop if you don't get home
by midnight but you or your marriage might.

You have not had one over the limit. The car
just passing my window at twice the speed
of sound wants to get home before he left.
But you are sensible of speed and direction,
like the coffee served in Little Chefs.
Today I have been nowhere important, seen
no one I know. Realism takes the day off;

language isn't restricted, it's in code. 'Coffee
please,' means, 'Let me out of this town, I think
they're watching me.' Not so much paranoia
as an awareness of cameras. Last night I saw
your car on *Police: Camera: Action*, leaving
the scene of an accident. No one was hurt,
it was a near thing and you weren't involved.

You were only passing the flashing lights
of breakdown service vans, thinking of Sales
and your wife's face turned away. Outside,
I hear the bang of a door, a car starting,
moving off into the main road and away.

National Express

Still dark. Middle of winter, not even.
You would have caught a taxi but.
Early to rise workers with donkey jackets,
a woman with Metro stitched to her coat.

So you get to the station and the coach.
Made it. The driver tears the top
off your ticket and you climb.
Sets off through dew-wet streets:

garage, charity shop, 'A Cut Above',
shuttered: 'The American Diner'. You're
going to meet you're not going to meet
the Queen. The capital of this once great.

So here's Stockport and by now it's still
dark but maybe. More get on. It's not
till the motorway you see the sky:
pearl grey. Not that the sun exactly.

But the day spreads over the land like.
On your way to the [traffic at Birmingham].

The Trouble With Being A Dog

Dragged through all weathers,
a stiff breeze round the park
and the rain – dogged persistence
every day for a month. I'd give

my canines to sniff that setter's
glorious behind. Leashed together
we go by the boating lake
with ducks then some sad wreck

breaks up my reverie of barks:
'Is she yours?' Soft lad says,
'I'm walking him for a friend,'
and the weather turns historic,

still, old codger smells of pee.
I'm expected to lick his hand
(tastes of cardboard) so I do.
We gather our personal clouds:

'Look after her, I lost my own,'
and he's off like he's seen,
the other side of the lake,
something that used to be his.

After Wordsworth

I was aimless in Leeds, walking
the streets back of the gallery
in a weatherfront of wind
and fine rain, when I happened on
a pair of enormous arms held out
to dance with the air; that morning

my head went walkabout from a
dull sobbing draughty flat. It caught
the next bus out of Manchester
and only started to cheer up
late afternoon when I saw two
reaching arms on a stripey pole.

As the dusk muscled in, water
in Mandela Gardens sparkled
grimly but I declined to accept
its offer of a waltz round town.
On the coach later I wondered
if I'd ever felt at home in

this, or that other universe
I've imagined but not lived in.

New York, Paris

Somebody's just had toast. The newsreader's voice
walks over headlines in comfortable shoes,

and I'm looking at my shelves, wondering
how I'd take all these books if I left.

I've always wanted to live in 50's New York
or Paris at the dawn of the twentieth:

not the Bateau Lavoir but near enough
to smell the fresh paint on a Picasso.

The door to the living room's open. A smiley face
is blu-tacked to the glass. In a year's time

I might be somewhere else. New York or Paris
or even Barcelona in the 80's, or now.

Lunch Poem

Last time I met Frank he was eating
a burger and fries in Waterstones Deansgate.
I was getting into a cheese pasty

from Gregg's, Cross St, and told him off in the Art
Department for coming between Matisse
and Picasso. Though I was walking with my head

in a book at the time he apologised:
'I've got all these words and nothing to write on'
but didn't he tell me once he'd strolled

to the Times Square typewriter store,
put a sheet in the first Olivetti at
exactly 12:20 in New York, a Friday.

Starting With A Line By Declan MacManus

There's still pretty insults left
among the weather of a summer
that's had trouble starting. Magpies
waking the dead or the chi-chi Walkman
slowly deafening the man with the headphones
in the post office queue or as you enter
the Holy Land of Manchester Central Ref
I'm reminded of a book I'd forgotten, things
I should have done yesterday but put off.

Stop there! That never happened, or if it did
only in my head. How it was, or is: the chance
coming together of grammar and syntax.
Meeting you was meeting a small neat storm
in a desert: refreshing but startling. Late
for your birthday but here at last, a train
delayed by epiphanies: inside the skull
the wakeful brain decides to enjoy the ride,
so keep your hands inside the dodgems

and don't let go the bar. A robin in a nest
engages in a little garden philosophy:
we talk life, cabbages and slugs, how any
moment you could be interrupted
and the last line's waiting when you
get home. Leave dogs to bark, don't
explain a single comma of your life,
even in the bluest noonday of July.

Mobile

It's not true till it's on TV
but I could do with a mobile phone
so that when something happens
like this, you can tell me
it's on all five channels and Sky

and for once in my life I'll be
in on the ground floor,
not thinking it's a hoax and
how grand it would be to blow
the whole capitalist caboodle

sky high. I'll start to feel bad
when the body count rises,
but now I'm remembering the times
I put God on trial and dreamed
of his overthrow as a tyrant

who didn't exist. That was before
I got religious and learned
nothing was ever that simple;
now my friends get the updates
but we have a deadline to meet

as we set up the camera and I
stroll across a bowling green
again and again and again.

Night Before

The living room a chaos
of paper and books. We
explore each other's skin
my tongue in your mouth

not knowing what to say.
I stop myself falling
into your breasts, hands
from wandering between

your legs. I don't know,
to believe your eyes see
no one but me? Fear like
an animal cornered by an

open cage, messier than
the life I've drifted through
so long. I want it and I
don't till by the door as you

leave you touch me, there;
hours later awake in the dark
a light clicks on: I'll never
switch it off, this is love
and won't let me go.

The Cloud People

Tonight on TV a people who live among clouds.
Love comes knocking, I don't let her in. Peruvian
forests with seven-necked snakes keep out the curious.
Love keeps knocking but I'm not in, moved away,
on an urgent mission elsewhere in this jungle.
They tied hands over the eyes of their dead
as if the suns of Paradise would blind them.
The noise gets louder: love knocks at midnight,
won't take refusal, breaks and enters my house,
my head, pillows won't keep her out. The world's
largest archeological dig is a city lost, found then
lost and found again: walls, impossibly huge, rise
like giants shaking the sleep from their eyes.

I wake to knocking: love at the window waits
to be let in. The programme's over before
it begins; I dream a people wandering through trees,
mist a poncho round mysterious tall shoulders.
I'm afraid of my mail; love comes knocking with
a message for my heart. Looters have ransacked
the tombs; once they would climb for a chat,
to sort a problem with debt, pay respects. Now
love climbs through my window, rearranges my furniture,
leaves it exactly the same except for
the knowledge she's here. They disappeared
back to the clouds, the moon, left hieroglyphs, walls,
their dead in caves. Love knocks me from my chair,
I can't catch my breath. I want to live
with these people of air.
Love knocks holes in the walls of my heart.
Come live with me in the mountains of Peru.

Figures

Those numbers in your
you mustn't forget. Buttons
pressed to get you through. Bank on it:
someone counts the hairs of your head.

Stars are not countless. Some head
somewhere has the precise figures
lodged in its cells. Ten
to the power of. Your PIN number

swallows your card: refer
to bank. All the dumped
numerals crashed, gone down, forgot.
Her phone number, bastard, a blank.

Who invented zero? You
right now: big O the shape
of a mouth. Arabs were first,
or the Vedas: you forget.

Accosted By Angels

The day he was lost among warehouses
at the back of the market, these
Jesus loves you eyes invited him to church.

He said no because he already went,
could never shake that certainty that stuck
and glued him together like Cow Gum,
but he wants us to know that at the time
he was trying to live in the world
though not at that moment succeeding.

*Sometimes, I disappear for weeks
from under my own nose, and I should
have been cleaning house for her return,
I should have been thinking of her.*

Instead, he was dragged from his dream
by a tract in his hand, *If you change your mind* …
then back wherever he went when the road
grew too uncomfortable. I never understood
that side of him: one minute here, the next

off with the fairies having some dispute
with himself: like he asked one day:
if God is a question what is the answer?
I said, *Don't quote metaphysics,
now go and say sorry, and mean it.*

You Hated The Film

and so did I: thought
it would be great till it all
went wrong: too late for popcorn,

sneaking in: time dragged
deeper and deeper
into its own furrow.

Good film, bad date
getting worse. It just
went on: characters

got nasty, nastier, and no
redemption as I saw you
draw further back to the life

you'd come to escape.
The film days from its end,
we could have left, let's

call this our turkey; but so
well made: those shots
of the bay, the costumes,

dialogue to die for; tension
wound up in stages: I'd write
the review, give it five stars

then hate it like you do.

Tired

1
Not the stones of her eyes
but the stiff of her shoulder

Not the slowness of step
but the lead in her shoes

The wall of her back
when he tries to touch her:

the news is bad in the café
as he clears old cups,

goes for latte and cakes.

2
He'd like to lift that pack
of worries, let her sleep.

But this is not
her refuge in the States;

and there's plenty of time
in the universe but she

must leave for the Metro,
return to people coming

as he walks round the space
in his life most loving her.

3
He could watch her all night

just sleeping, hear her breath

take flight and land
like a bumble bee

that shouldn't fly
but does, could watch

till light filters in
through the curtains

but she opens her eyes
I have to go and they're

all efficiency
to get her home.

Shifting Furniture

I've learned to cup her left breast
without fear in my hand. I've learned
to take time, not be afraid of the hurt
that in any case isn't there
to speak of. I listen at two in
the morning for the shift of
furniture over my head. She always
goes and she always comes back,
I always understand. That banging
in the upstairs flat never stops.
To think I nearly lost her through
carelessness, through my own
deliberate fault. I ought to bang on
the ceiling, make cocoa if I'd any milk,
wish we were sleeping off love,
waking at dawn when the moon
dissolves in puddles like aspirin
after the night before.

Simple

Late as usual, she comes in from the car.
He makes coffee in the cafetière
bought to impress with. *Do you
know what we share?* she asks.

Reaching for the blood and breath
of each other: he thought he had
complexes. He grows less clever
when he sheds his clothes, wears

his own body round the flat.
She makes mincemeat of his
hidden depths, breathes in time
with the 4/4 beat in his chest.

The last train rumbles in the distance
like a muffled clock: they dress,
rush out to kiss by the car
she's still absurdly proud of.

What do we share? A bass drum
thuds in his head, oh yes, he knows.

Like The First Morning

Clouds wagon-trail west in sky like a ski slope
as the bloke round the back sleeps on in his flat.
Get up, and you remember last night, her voice
so low it brushed the floor like a skirt. Still night,
      it's time to be up and about.

Tune in the radio: news slides like warm milk frothing
from speakers. Daylight seeps through windows that can't
open their eyes. Sometimes, love's a pain in the neck
you'll never get enough of. Where's that new shirt?
      – it's time to be up and about.

And have you written her name in god's list of
things to do: cut her some slack? Now you'll worry
for her all day but still go to work. Are all
your lessons prepared? Drink up your coffee
      – it's time you were up and about.

Ironing Your Top

I can't quite reach the frown of cloth
that stays unsmoothed under the arm.
But you would know how to do collars,
make a single line down the crease
of a pair of washable trousers.
I just run it along, press the steam button,

flatten T-shirts one after the other.
Jazz keeps me going: Chet Baker, Bill Evans,
crisp as white shirts hung in the wardrobe
for interviews. At your place,
soft rock eases over the board
simple as this top I've always loved

because it slips so beautifully off.

Every Day Is Like Sunday

drifts down from the bedroom ceiling
as I draw invisible lines down your spine
to the small oxbow of sweat at the base.

'Please Please Please Can I Get What I Want'
from the couple above. You stay
for a couple of hours but the ghost
of Givenchy hangs round all day.
Let's doze if they'll let us
but 'The Boy With A Thorn In His Side'

is playing as you dress and go
leaving the taste of salt on my tongue.
By now they've reached 'The Queen Is Dead'
and you'll be playing the tape
I made for your car as my finger
paints the outline of your face
on the woodchip walls of my room.

When they come to the inevitable breakups
and solo careers, I'll get up, unable to stand
all this happiness, and open the curtains
with nothing but you in my head
and 'This Charming Man'.

Letters To The Editor
'Correspondence on this matter is now closed'

PATIENTLY WAITING

Is there anyone out there can help?
It's been twenty years since I crashed
into your city, I have a good job,
pay taxes. Just because I'm not

from round here, my skin's green and
my eyes deep red (see photo) is no
reason to run. I never intended to invade
or bring you a message of peace.

Are you blonde/brunette/redhead?
Will you tolerate my little ways?
The little finger on my left hand
won't bend: which could prove useful

if you know what I mean. Would
anyone out there care to meet
this lovesick shipwrecked alien?
I promise to spin tales of my stars

till you fall asleep in my arms.
Please write (enclosing photo) to
the Box No. below. All serious
offers considered. Please write soon.

La Vache Enragé

Our favourite read's your cookery page
with your *Recipes for Unemployed Cooks.*
We've already tried most of them out;
tonight is Baked Beans and Whiskas.

Your *Recipes for Unemployed Cooks*
have proved really popular with our lot:
tonight it's Baked Beans and Whiskas,
basted in lashings of curry. But the dish

that's proved most popular with our lot
is Arse of Mad Cow Stuffed with Acorns,
basted in lashings of curry, dished up
after baking for hours in the oven.

Arse of Mad Cow Stuffed with Acorns
goes well with your Daffodil Salad;
after baking it for hours in the oven
we wash it down with cheap hock:

goes well with your Daffodil Salad.
To each meal add touches of luxury,
so we wash it down with cheap hock
that can deaden the bitterest taste.

To each meal add touches of luxury,
so everything's drowned in cheap booze
that can deaden the bitterest taste.
We'll sit down to fags and the paper

when everything's drowned in cheap booze.
Will there be another instalment

as we sit down to fags and the paper?
Your recipes are really nutritious,

will there be another instalment?
We've already tried most of them out;
your recipes are really nutritious.
Our favourite read's your cookery page.

Grateful Citizen

Thank you for that piece on our radiant streets.
Though some of the detail was wrong, it was
a fine piece of writing. You made me believe

I lived among piazzas, roadside restaurants,
enchanting temples; not this heap of burnt
estates. The statues littering boulevards

gleam like distant memories of the times
I walked these streets among the detritus
of charity shopping. I pictured that slow river

lined with trees and walkways where folk
gathered to eat sandwiches, chat about culture
and the many varieties of goods available

in even the lowliest of stores; it may be muggers' alley
but still it's a dream. I'm glad you were there
to describe the invisible treasures of our history,

What fine descriptions of the ranks
of heroic miners and dockers on street corners,
singing arias from tragic operas, selling flowers,

matches, cigarette lighters to finance the novels
they are certainly writing in bedsits. Thank you
for describing the weather, the storms and sunlight,

that replaced our usual drizzle. In my heart I believe
every word, learn it by heart and, having sent you
this letter, shall, I assure you, pluck out my eyes.

Ornithologist

Am I the first to report this?
I walked my schnauzer by
the overspill estate and thought
I heard the distinctive call
of the Common Glottal Stop,

the t', t' of the newly hatched
rising in a chorus of clicks
from some secret nesting site.
Your readers may think it
extinct since the influx of

louder varieties; but though
it's never seen I often hear its
rooftop caesura as if it were
no more than a doorstep away.
Such music is surely worth

preserving on these streets.
Unlike most threatened fauna
this bird of dun camouflage
still leaves a space for itself
language can't fill. Today

I thought I'd found one feather
of our most ubiquitous bird
that nests in forests of housing,
where it's known chiefly for a song
dropped through a crack in the throat.

Blue Forever

I write in response to your article on favourite colours.
Mine contains in it all shades from sea and sky
to the shirt my favourite daughter bought for me
this Christmas, which I wear every day.

I own a cobalt Sierra, some years old, dashboard
cyan, seat covers slate. My furniture's royal,
cerulean, pale; my carpet's dyed turquoise
and peacock. I drink every week in the Oxford.

Even the jeans that hug the hips of the lovely ladies
at the shop where I purchase my baccy, or the bags
of salt in my crisps, are stained that inestimable hue.
Not everything I own is thus tinted; though the tiles

in my bathroom gleam ultramarine, the towels
are crimson, a gift from the wife I divorced
due to being incompatible. Some years ago I joined
a club of ancient Celtic enthusiasts. Each weekend

in the summer we paint our bodies in woad
and charge naked over hills at Romans in gold and
silver accoutrements. Elmore James
picks a fine twelve bars on bottleneck steel

as I wrap myself in whisky haze to keep
my melancholia in check. I am neither obsessed
nor an anorak, as last night's correspondent implied.
You may well find he too favours some reckless

shade of opinion, and no one accuses him;
though I have often thought such pigments
predisposed one to tempers, hot flushes
and problems with the heart; where I am
calm, pacific, a sea rolling azure forever.

Make-Over

He looked around, saw life gathered in piles
neat as clothes in drawers. Outside,
the car in its driveway waiting to go.
Bottles lined windowsills, Royal Doulton
cracked in cupboards. A silent radio
on the sideboard. Then he found himself

in her chair. Her hat was on the arm
so he wore it. Slowly at first, clumsy,
he changed into knickers, bra, the black dress
she wore the day before. There was her make-up;
first he wiped it off, clownish, went slower.
Everything fitted; under the standard lamp

he almost mistook himself. Lipstick, mascara,
the thinnest eye-pencil. Then he set to
in the kitchen: he'd watched her for years,
he made tops sparkle, plates whistle.
Living room, bathroom, master bedroom;
and at the end he went to the car, sat

in the passenger and looked in the mirror,
saw her, expecting to be home by midnight.

The Suitcase

is tired of standing in hallways.
Would like please to be returned
to the cupboard under the stairs,
emptied of that one grey suit,
shirts still wrapped in brown paper
and socks rolled up into balls.

What's it doing with all that cash,
in high-denomination notes
stuffed in a pigskin wallet
between The Gentleman's Travel Kit,
the long johns and the vests?

It's sick of playing these guessing games,
what's in the secret compartment,

and as for the smiles of the dead,
it carries these in a box with the shoes
(scuffed, worn down at the heels.)
Maybe, if you could find yourself
washing off the dust from roads
that no longer lead anywhere,

it could stop standing in hallways,
grandad, watching the door.

Lost

I'm looking for my voice. Have you found it?
I left it on the bus: did you take it home
by mistake instead of your own?

I must find it now I've so much to say.
I thought if I put it out it would be back

but I'm worried sick, it's been weeks,
not a word. Did you pick it up
with shopping or luggage? Is it

languishing in cupboards or drawers,
waiting for speech at the back of your garage
with the tyres and Playboys?

Was it caged against its will, throat cut,
with those terrible dreams? It's out there,
calling my name, I can't wake up.

Grey

is a kind of bored colour chart
on slumped serge shoulders
talking about the weather and gardening.

finds his father staring from mirrors
each morning at eight, his hair
eroding like coastlines in the rain.

is a long dull evening
that keeps re-reading
the same few books
the same dreams of a war zone
that smells of polish
and school-dinner custard.

has a love affair with bread, nearly stale
in the packet, could stand a year and a day
with hands in his pockets at the bar
discussing the diseases of roses.

is a pair of spectacles that can see
in black and white but can't
even manage a good black dog.

A Sea Change
after Stephen Jay Gould

Much occupied by God, our Captain
relates the wonder of divine order:
each creature in its place, from ant
to master and his slaves, sailing the ship
of species through the faithless sea:

examples finches, their beaks,
variegated. Charles, the perfect
gentleman, listens as his desire
to take cloth slips off his shoulders
like an oldfashioned cloak.

Later, in his bunk, he speculates
on the shape of a turtle's shell. Such
evidence will wreck good Fitzroy,
strand his craft on some deserted shore
all hands lost as the SS Evolution

ploughs through an ocean of facts.
Our Captain waves the Good Book, sees
the future steam away from him,
Admiral Darwin at the helm
and crews of apes in the engine room.

Early Communion

In these traffic free hours birds have to themselves
uncalled for sun invades your room,
intones the words not quite remembered or defined:
you step outside and faith seems possible, walk

to church where what seemed lost
breaks the day's wafer over your head. Afterwards
you trail through puddles of the night before
as if dropped leaves had blessed each stride

though nothing's changed, only shifted slightly
round a curve in space; you're still dragging heels
but caught in that exposing light that drinks
you in and will not ever let you go.

Godtalk

Right into the middle of a conversation
he drops the word God. We were talking
about yoga and karma and reincarnation
when he just happens to mention it.

Would you step on me if I came back as an ant ?
It was like something dragged in by the cat,
undoubtedly dead with something dribbling
from the side of its mouth. I wouldn't mind

coming back as a cat. Nothing to do all day
but eat sleep crap. Would you have me done
if I came back as a cat? He's the sort
who would mention God in the middle
of a conversation: I bet in a previous life

he was a sideboard, if I asked him his sign
he'd probably say Blue Nun. I met a girl once
claimed she was Josephine. Could we pollinate
if I came back as a bee and you as a rose?

The man who mentioned God has the picture
of a golfer on his jumper, and doesn't play golf.

Seen The Light

> *'As he neared Damascus on his journey, suddenly a light from heaven flashed around him.'* Acts 9.3

Was it out of the blue? – a Kodak flash
introduced itself like gravity no light
escapes from I was scared like a weight
lifted did you know what to do with it?

I couldn't drive because I was blind but
are you coming or not so I came and
how was my life supposed to change
after coffee and biscuits and a room

of nets and metaphors I couldn't see
for days my tongue hanging on a word
that didn't come all I could think of
was help and my life turned round

how was it for you? ever since I've
sat in my car tried to figure it
even went to church sat at the back
but they were talking something foreign

so I left.

Room With A View

Light outside my bedroom at midnight
is not the moon. When I wake up with a line,
when someone walks past the sensor,
and the room turns confessional, searchlights
bed, chair, clothes draped over the furniture,

I miss you with the same ache
as when the light came from the porch,
left on that first night after you'd gone
and I couldn't sleep, couldn't think,
till I'd switched it off before writing you.

Sometimes I use this time for prayer,
when there's nothing for it but to get in touch
with the centre, or invite this loneliness
to spend the night, put my books on shelves,
tidy my flat till I'm sleepy as the light blinks.

In the living room, everything's huge.

Desire Paths

Barely two minutes after the turf's laid
a rough diagonal of muddy footprints
triangulates the lawn. I made the grade
and almost knew where the words went

ploughing through sentences: felt a foot
taller as I walked. Is this how it feels,
I thought over coffee in the pub where I sat
eating lunch. The world rides on its rails;

now as I arrive by tram, my desire
strides over council grass to meet me,
blind to the signposts flaming everywhere.
These moments travel with us, set us free

as when you first stepped out on a shortcut
across my best-laid plans, my new-mown heart.

On Light:

how sometimes when I've felt
all week like one flickering bulb
left on in the house, you creep
through the creaking door
at the back of my head like

you've just got in tiptoeing
from a party upstairs, and
I hear you bang pans in the kitchen,
make something out of scraps
from last night's fading conversations,

as birdsong starts out the back
and a kettle comes to the boil.